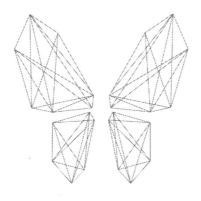

the i in life

SARA DELPASAND

ARCHWAY
PUBLISHING

Illustrator of the butterfly wings: Amber Patino
Cover art was created by Andres Ernesto Acosta, a
designer and consultant in Los Angeles

Archway Publishing books may be ordered through booksellers or by contacting:

Archway Publishing
1663 Liberty Drive
Bloomington, IN 47403
www.archwaypublishing.com
1 (888) 242-5904

ISBN: 978-1-4808-4174-1 (sc)
ISBN: 978-1-4808-4175-8 (hc)
ISBN: 978-1-4808-4176-5 (e)

Library of Congress Control Number: 2017901703

Print information available on the last page.

Archway Publishing rev. date: 4/24/2017

To Mihan: Thank you for awakening my "I" in life. I wish you were here.

To my family: You are my motivation, my bliss, my all.

Contents

Introduction

If I had known then what I know now...

Imagine that you could have a heart-to-heart talk with your younger self. Envision looking at yourself in the mirror and seeing the reflection of your younger self wearing your favorite outfit from back in the day, rocking the hairstyle of that time while listening to the tunes from that era that you still connect with and that bring out all of your memories from the past. What would you see if you could take a look at the person you left in the past, but who is still so much a part of you today? And if you could, in that moment, give your younger self a piece of advice, what would it be?

Would you say,

> "Don't take life too seriously"?
> "Everything will be okay"?
> "You are good enough"?
> "Believe in yourself"?
> "Work harder"?
> "Study more"?
> "Laugh more"?
> "Stress less"?

How would that conversation play out?

I was asked that question some time ago, and it made me reminisce about the past. This reminiscing awakened a lot of memories, both good and bad. I had so much to tell my younger self about life. I wished I'd had more clarity on my *I* earlier in life—meaning the *me* without the physical aspect. So, I dedicated the next two years of my life to writing this book to my younger self.

My intention was to provide clarity for my inner youth, to give a better sense of why I am who I am today. If I had known then what I know now, I would have lived my life knowing that I was put on this earth to serve and give, not just to take. I was born being me, who I am, and my talents and abilities are unique for a reason. All I have to do in life is specify my talents and qualities, figure out how and in what ways they can benefit others, and start serving that purpose. What a great sense of relief I have knowing that the purpose of my existence is not for me to fill myself up with what the world has to offer but to empty myself into the world.

This book is meant to inspire you to identify your *I* in life by recognizing your talents, core values, and goals, and aligning them with your greatest strengths, so you can serve your purpose. With the right tools and exercises to gain clarity on yourself and what you are truly passionate about, you can take charge and be in control of your own destiny.

God knows how many times I've stopped to check myself so far in life, and I have no doubt that I will do so a couple more times on my journey. This one is for you, so that at any stage of your life, you can stop and center yourself by getting a clear sense of who you are, where you are going, and how you will get there.

This book is divided into four chapters. The first chapter is a letter to my younger self, in which I share my philosophy on a way of life that has helped me center my *I* in life. It's about understanding the connection to the self, and therefore to all. It will help you realize that we are here to give, not just take. The question is not so much what I want to do but more how I can serve using my talents, values, skills, and interests. I want you to *feel* this part of the book, not think it.

Chapter two, three and four presents hands-on exercises that will guide you in the search for your purpose and career path. With the right set of tools, you can gain clarity on your values, goals, and your

I in life. This part of the book will serve as your own professional diary. Take your time going through each exercise, and remember that this is based on who you are today. The intention behind this part of the book is not only to specify what your values, skills, interests and talents are but also how you can use them professionally—and most importantly, *why* you should use them professionally.

A shift in awareness is needed to make the world a better place. I believe that such a shift can come from being enlightened by your individual purpose. I work on my personal growth and becoming aligned with my purpose, with the intention of inspiring others around me. I wish the same for you. You can bring awareness and clarity to this world only once you have brought it to yourself.

I believe that we are all one energy. The same sensation you feel throughout your veins at this exact moment, I feel in my veins. I feel the vibrating sensation of the divine, and it brings a smile to my face knowing that I am not alone. I see you and feel your presence. Thank you for being here.

I dedicate this book to all of our younger selves in the pursuit of living life to the fullest.

Chapter 1

The Letter

I am not afraid… I was born to do this. – Jeanne d'Arc

A Letter to My Younger Self

If I could live life all over again, knowing what I know today, would I live it differently? If I could do it all over again—go back and lay where you are sleeping and wake up the next morning knowing what I know today—would I think differently? Since I cannot go back in time, I will slip this letter of life under your pillow in the hope that you will wake up in the morning and find it, and continue the divine journey of life with ease and purpose.

Dear *I*,

I know you are lying in bed, looking up, reminiscing about the past school year, and smiling as all the great memories play out like a movie projected on the ceiling. It's June 8th—your eighteenth birthday. Congratulations on being a good friend! You have so many friends, and they seem to appreciate you and love being around you. You are doing well in school, even though you are skipping a few classes to hang out with your friends at the mall. Your family adores you—your dad, mom, and sister. You truly are blessed.

Now, you probably want to know who I am. Well, I am you, about ten years from now, and this is my "cheat note" of life to you. I am so happy to be able to talk to you; I've been wanting to for so long. I think about you all the time, my teenage warrior. You bring out the fighter in me. I recall your attitude and sassiness whenever I question myself, as I too often do as an adult. Thank you for speaking your mind and always being so inquisitive. I really love it when you tell it like it is. You have set a firm foundation for me to build on.

I know it's hard to be young, trying to convey the perfect image of life and create the image you *think* is the real you. It's hard going through high school, dealing with day-to-day drama and feeling insecure about everything that happens between you, your friends, and your family. I see why you have become a people pleaser; it is easier that way. You feel like if you're not perfect in every way, you're not doing it right. Your looks have to be perfect; you have to talk right, sit right, do right, be right, or you will fail to live up to the image society and those around you have established as the ultimate ambition.

Since you do not yet understand what is the most valuable part of you—the non-physical, internal you, which you can feel, but can't see—you will dedicate your life to everything that is external, trying to achieve perfection. Since perfection is unattainable (as you realized early on in life), your fear of failure will prevent you from giving it your all, so that you won't disappoint yourself or anyone else. It is easier that way, and you will continue to choose the easy path for a few more years.

You will go to college, where you will be passionate about your studies, but will not give one hundred percent. You will move out of your parents' house and settle down because you think life is that simple. You will get a job that you will thrive in, but it will feed your insecurities, because you will question your skills and every decision you make, worried that they're not perfect. There will be moments when you will be aligned with your purpose, but will fail to recognize and appreciate the achievement of serving your talent, because you are not awakened to your *I* in life.

When you are clear on who you are, where you are going, and how you will get there, you will have an awakening. When you act on that awakening of clear intention and purpose, you will be aligned with the divine, and the fear of not being good enough will subside.

So, let's start the journey of getting to know your *I* in life. I am not here to change you. I love who you are, and I am so proud that you are a part of me and I am a part of you. I am here to bring awareness to your *I*. Your *I* is your purpose, and it feeds your soul. I will describe it as best I can, but I need you to feel this part, not think it.

The *I* in "God"

*Stand up straight and realize who you are, that you
tower over your circumstances. You are a child of
God. Stand up straight.* – Maya Angelou

Feel Your Soul

In order to find your purpose in life, you have to get to know who you are and why you are here. There is no definitive answer, as it will change when you evolve in life. Rather than a perfect image that you must match, it is more of a connection for you to *feel*.

You will never understand yourself until you learn to feel God—the infinite energy that institutes patterns of creation in all shapes and forms, including space, the universe, planets, and earth. All of these are different manifestations of God, as are you. You are one with God through your soul, your spirit, and your inner light. Your soul is an extension of God, and to be *of* God means that you have certain attributes in common. It is your duty to recognize this and act accordingly. One attribute is the power of creation. Let that thought sink in for a minute or two.

You are a co-creator with God, here to maintain the best existence you can imagine and fulfill your excellence by working and serving diligently to help build a better world. Allow your divinity to empower you, for you are not a coincidence but a fingerprint of God—the infinite energy of all there is. Maybe you're not society's perception of perfection, but being one with God puts society's view to shame.

Embrace Your Body

Your body is your soul's temple. Your soul and body are united, but not joint. This means that the soul can leave the body, but remains aligned with it throughout your life. When the soul is no longer meant to shine through the body, it parts from it. Like any flower that blooms, the body is here to share its beauty, strength, and divinity for a period of time. When it has fulfilled its purpose, it departs.

Your body is a manifestation of God in physical form and is guided by your soul. You are godlike and have divine powers. You could say that are you are a real-life Superwoman or Superman. Every second of every minute of every hour of every day, your body is making magic happen.

Let's take your mind, for example: It can perform a quadrillion operations per second without you even knowing it. It's making hundred gallons of blood per hour flow through your veins with a precise amount of pressure. It's making your heart beat right now, and it's maintaining your body's core temperature to keep you alive. All of this is done by your subconscious mind; this is how powerful you are. If you lie still for a minute and close your eyes, you will be able to feel the divine force of energy pulsating through your veins, beating in your chest, and filling up your lungs. Talk about perfection!

The *I* in Humanity

Stop acting so small. You are the universe in ecstatic motion. – Rumi

Free Your Mind

You create as you think, speak, and act. You can create negatively (causing misery, fear, and revenge) or positively (creating harmony, confidence, and joy). You can make this life heaven or hell depending on how you think, speak, and act. If your thoughts, words, and actions are positive, you will create your own heaven on earth by bringing harmony and love to your surroundings. And if your thoughts, words, and actions are negative, you will create a hell on earth, where you will experience misery and despair.

Your thought patterns cause your feelings. To master your mind and body, you must understand how your mind works. Your thoughts produce a biochemical reaction in your brain, which then releases chemical signals. These signals act like messengers that are transmitted to the body. It is thoughts that produce the chemicals in the brain that allow your body to feel the way you were just thinking.

So, when you think happy or positive thoughts, your brain produces a chemical called dopamine that shifts the brain and body, making you feel uplifted and excited. If you have negative or self-destructive thoughts, your brain produces chemicals called neuropeptides that cause you to feel angry or unworthy. Words and thoughts create experiences. This illustrates a simple teaching that has been practiced for thousands of years: good thoughts, good words, and good deeds. It is as simple as that.

Your soul is good—pure divinity, positive and bright—so, whenever your mind shifts to negative thoughts, just change your thoughts to support the idea of feeling good. This will re-align your mind with your soul. Alignment of mind, body, and soul is the ultimate achievement, and it can be reached through the experience of life.

Discover Your Purpose

Your soul evolves through experience, and that is how we serve our purpose. We are here to experience feelings throughout our lives. The only thing we can do is be in the present, which is the now—feeling love and joy, the way we do when we see a newborn baby; feeling proud when we see our beloved succeed; or feeling pain when we mourn the passing of a loved one. To do this, we must feel the vibrations of life and recognize them for what they are, good or bad. All we have is the now, and when life happens, our thoughts and reactions are the primary cause of the outcome, for better or worse.

When something bad happens in your life or in the world, do not reinforce negative vibes by focusing on them and contemplating how things should've, could've, or would've been. Take a moment to look at the situation and see it for what it really is. You can understand your situation better by remaining in the present and practicing the art of pure observation that is not clouded by fear, judgment, anxiety, and expectation.

Clarify for yourself why the situation is affecting you in a negative way. Honor the existence of each thought and then free yourself from it by releasing the weight of sadness and worry. Always focus on and reinforce what excites you. Spread positivity by sharing thoughts and words of good things in this life. You can only end the suffering around you by spreading what you want the outcome to be. If you want love, then act on love: show love, speak of love, and be love. If you want peace, then act on peace: show peace, speak of peace, and be peace. You can never do any good if you act on hatred, show hatred, and speak of hatred, for you will become hatred. The equation is that simple. Good thoughts = good words = good deeds.

As we live, we fulfill our soul's purpose by serving our talent. We serve by mastering our thoughts, words, and actions to create an alliance with our purpose. When we are aligned with our purpose and act on it, we are sharing the essence of God.

Human beings who are aligned with their divine purpose, no matter how much adversity they face, will bring harmony to this world. Rumi, Mother Theresa, the Dalai Lama, Oprah Winfrey, Michelangelo, Martin Luther King Jr, Albert Einstein, Nelson Mandela, Joan of Arc, da Vinci, doctors, caregivers, teachers, artists, and all others who have ever had some kind of positive impact on the world have all had one thing in common: They were all aligned with their soul's purpose and shared it with their existence.

The *I* in the Gift

Your talent is God's gift to you. What you do with
it is your gift back to God. – Leo Buscaglia

Find Your Talent

In order to live your purpose, you have to do what excites your soul. You can also call it talent. You were born with it; it is part of your divinity. You might think that you don't have a talent, but that is impossible.

We all have a talent that we were born with, and we serve our purpose in life by sharing it with existence. Someone around you has mentioned your talent to you at some point in your life—a teacher, a parent, or a friend. Maybe you have a beautiful voice, an eye for design, a knack for math or physics, a gift for sports, or dance moves comparable to MJ's.

What thrilled you as a child? What made those moments enjoyable, and what were the common threads? What makes you lose track of time? What do you yearn to do? By now, you probably think that communication might be one of your talents, because you enjoy talking with your friends and they confide in you—and you are right. You have been using your talent in many different ways, even as a child.

Remember when you were only nine and spent the whole year in woodshop class making a "real" school desk for your little sister, so you could teach her how to read and write over the summer, before she started school? Remember when you were eleven and you implemented a one-hour "family talk" every Sunday, so you could connect with your mom, dad, and sister, and talk about what was going on in their lives and yours? And in high school, remember when you started mentoring groups for the girls in your sister's class, so that you could indirectly coach your sister through puberty? Communication thrilled you, and you would figure out creative ways to implement it in your life. Your talent and passion will become the foundation and the first step to serving your purpose, as your soul has been, and will always yearn, to serve this purpose to feel complete.

Every one of God's creations is fulfilling its purpose. Take a flower, for example. It blooms and shares its pollen and beauty until it wilts and fades away, reuniting with the creator. Animals do the same; they serve their abilities and talents for the greater good of their flock. Ants are a great example of serving for the greater good. Each ant has a specific task, based on its talent, that it uses to get food, build the anthill, protect its queen, and so on. All creatures exist to serve in one way or another. So, on our journey, we are obligated to do the same—to find our talents and share them with the intention of serving the greater good.

Know this: Life is a journey, and an incredible one. But it will only become what you make of it. There is no need to feel pressure; I want you to take a minute and feel empowered. Good or bad, you are in charge. All there is to it is to explore your talent and passion and share them with your family, neighborhood, community, country, or the world. Regardless of the scale, you are here to share and serve the greater good. Do your best. That is all you can do.

The nature of your soul is to find its purpose before it unites with all. It will never settle; you will feel a void until the day you are aligned with your purpose and talent. The sooner you connect with your inner truth, light, soul, and talent, the sooner you can start sharing your divinity with ease and purpose.

The *I* in the Journey

Life is a journey, not a destination. – Ralph Waldo Emerson

The Act

No matter what life brings, do not lose the connection with your *I*. Deepen your connection every day by practicing the following exercises for a healthy and balanced life:

- **Practice gratitude.** Do this every day before you go to sleep or when you wake up in the morning. Close your eyes and feel the vibration in your chest as you think about and visualize everything that you are grateful for. Life is good!
- **Have faith and believe.** It does not matter what religion—who, when, or where. Just practice faith as often as you can. Stay connected to your God.
- **Go on a walk as often as you can.** Breathe in fresh air and enjoy the incredible manifestations of God.
- **Think of things that excite you and make you feel good.** Whenever a negative thought comes your way, replace it with a positive thought that makes you feel good. Focus on the good things in your life.
- **Use positive words every day.** Choose your words wisely. If you do not have anything constructive to say, do not say anything at all. Use your words to bring positive vibrations and energy to yourself and the people around you.
- **Perform an act of kindness every day.** Do something, small or big, to benefit someone else. Do it with the intention of sharing positive energy, and in a way that is aligned with your values and integrity. Help an elderly person carry groceries, walk the neighbor's dog, give seeds to the birds, hug someone who needs it, or give someone a gift. Smile; it gives you pleasure and brings pleasure to everyone around you.
- **Learn something new every day.** You can do this by reading a book or by simply talking and listening to a complete stranger about their talent, passion, and purpose. Get inspired! You never know where that knowledge and inspiration will lead.

- **Work on your craft.** Practice your talent every day, so that you can live up to your personal legend.
- **Get lucky!** Luck happens when preparation meets opportunity.
- **Talk to friends and family.** Develop deep relationships that allow you to share your thoughts and feelings. It is okay to be vulnerable. When you sit with a friend or a family member and share your thoughts, you will gain confidence by feeling how they accept you regardless of your fears and insecurities. When someone accepts you, it makes it easier for you to accept yourself. It is okay to be imperfect.

  By allowing friends and family space to share with you, you will also realize that everyone is facing challenges in life. Friends can give you perspective and clarity, helping you come to terms with the situations you encounter. This will empower you. Dare to talk about real things with your friends. After all, that is what they are there for: to witness and mirror you growing, learning, crying, and laughing.

  Trust the process of sharing. Step out of your comfort zone and embrace real friendships. Some people will not be able to handle this, but those who do will become blessings in your life. This kind of informal therapy is priceless, so do not get scared or discouraged when someone cannot be that kind of a friend to you. Keep sharing and believing until you find a good friendship match.

- **Pray!** Believe in the power of prayer. It is a positive practice to send vibrations of wishful thoughts and hopefulness to the universe. You will always receive what you pray for—maybe not in the shape or form you were expecting, but always aligned with your purpose.

- **Be healthy and take care of your body.** Your body houses your soul; nourish it. Be picky about what you eat. Keep in mind that you are obligated to take care of your body, but not to dedicate your sanity to it. A healthy body is one that is aligned with the mind and soul.

Know that you are not a coincidence but a purposeful being, and you are here to share your divinity. So, just recognize your talent— what you yearn to do and what comes naturally to you. Practice a healthy and positive way of life as you serve your purpose. Once you become aware of your *I*, you can start to serve it in accordance with your values and interests. Your talent in communication can be served in so many different ways; if your interests and values are aligned with politics, for example, you can choose a career path that will lead you in that direction. Complete the exercises in this book, and you will know what I know today and be aligned with your purpose, so that I can meet you in our awakening.

Chapter 2

Who am I?

Values

In order to achieve clarity on your purpose, it is essential to define what is important to you, what you value in life, what your interests are, and what your skills and abilities are.

Let's start by listing your values.

In the following list, place a checkmark next to each value that is important to you.

- ☐ Achievement
- ☐ Friendships
- ☐ Physical challenge
- ☐ Advancement and promotion
- ☐ Growth
- ☐ Pleasure
- ☐ Adventure
- ☐ Family
- ☐ Power and authority
- ☐ Affection (love and caring)
- ☐ Helping others
- ☐ Privacy
- ☐ Arts
- ☐ Public service
- ☐ Honesty
- ☐ Purity
- ☐ Change and variety
- ☐ Independence
- ☐ Close relationships
- ☐ Influencing others
- ☐ Community
- ☐ Inner harmony
- ☐ Recognition (respect from others, status)
- ☐ Competence
- ☐ Integrity
- ☐ Religion
- ☐ Competition
- ☐ Intellectual status
- ☐ Reputation
- ☐ Cooperation
- ☐ Involvement
- ☐ Responsibility and accountability
- ☐ My country
- ☐ Job tranquility
- ☐ Security
- ☐ Creativity
- ☐ Knowledge
- ☐ Self-respect

- ☐ Decisiveness
- ☐ Leadership
- ☐ Serenity
- ☐ Democracy
- ☐ Location
- ☐ Sophistication
- ☐ Ecological awareness
- ☐ Loyalty
- ☐ Stability
- ☐ Economic security
- ☐ Market position
- ☐ Status
- ☐ Effectiveness
- ☐ Meaningful work
- ☐ Supervising others
- ☐ Efficiency
- ☐ Accomplishment
- ☐ Time freedom
- ☐ Ethical practice

- ☐ Money
- ☐ Truth
- ☐ Excellence
- ☐ Nature
- ☐ Wealth
- ☐ Excitement
- ☐ Wisdom
- ☐ Fame
- ☐ Environment
- ☐ Stability
- ☐ Work under pressure
- ☐ Fast living
- ☐ Personal development
- ☐ Work with others
- ☐ Financial gain
- ☐ Freedom
- ☐ Working alone
- ☐ Animals
- ☐ My health

If there are values that are important to you that do not appear on the list above, you may add them below.

- ☐   ☐
- ☐   ☐

Choose eight key values and write them down in their order of importance to you.

1. _____

2. _____

3. _____

4. _____

5. _____

6. _____

7. _____

8. _____

Define these eight key values. What does each word mean to you? Be as specific as possible.

1. _____
_____
_____

2. _____
_____
_____

3. _____
_____
_____

4. _____
_____
_____

5. _____

_____

_____

6. _____

_____

_____

7. _____

_____

_____

8. _____

_____

_____

Describe how you can uphold each of your key values by applying them to your daily life and career.

1. _____

_____

_____

2. _____

_____

_____

3. _____

_____

_____

4. _____

_____

_____

5. _____

_____

_____

6. _____

_____

_____

7. _____

_____

_____

8. _____

_____

_____

Notes

Interests

Your interests arouse your enthusiasm and keep you curious. They play an important role in your happiness. It is important to pinpoint them and implement them in your daily life.

So, let's list your interests.

Place a checkmark next to each interest listed below that excites you.

- ☐ Forecasting
- ☐ Investigating
- ☐ Strategizing
- ☐ Producing/ Manufacturing
- ☐ Team building
- ☐ Inventing/Creating
- ☐ Tracking
- ☐ Forecasting
- ☐ Networking/Building relationships
- ☐ Coaching/Consulting
- ☐ Budgeting
- ☐ Purchasing
- ☐ Explaining
- ☐ Building/Constructing
- ☐ Questioning
- ☐ Testing
- ☐ Developing
- ☐ Categorizing
- ☐ Designing
- ☐ Repairing/Fixing
- ☐ Reading
- ☐ Watching TV
- ☐ Family time
- ☐ Fishing
- ☐ Computer
- ☐ Gardening
- ☐ Walking
- ☐ Exercising
- ☐ Music
- ☐ Entertaining
- ☐ Team sports
- ☐ Shopping
- ☐ Traveling
- ☐ Sleeping
- ☐ Socializing
- ☐ Fashion
- ☐ Coordinating
- ☐ Growing/Cultivating
- ☐ Innovating
- ☐ Calculating

- ☐ Animal care
  - ☐ Painting
  - ☐ Running
  - ☐ Dancing
  - ☐ Arranging
  - ☐ Inspecting/Examining
  - ☐ Assembling/Collecting
  - ☐ Marketing
  - ☐ Selling
  - ☐ Teaching/Training
  - ☐ Negotiating
  - ☐ Interviewing
  - ☐ Transporting/Driving
  - ☐ Serving
  - ☐ Collaborating
  - ☐ Problem solving
  - ☐ Analyzing
  - ☐ Advising/Consulting
  - ☐ Leading
  - ☐ Golf
  - ☐ Religious activities
  - ☐ Relaxing
  - ☐ Decorating
  - ☐ Crafts
  - ☐ Watching sports
  - ☐ Bicycling
  - ☐ Playing cards
  - ☐ Hiking
  - ☐ Cooking
  - ☐ Eating out
- ☐ Swimming
- ☐ Dating
- ☐ Camping
- ☐ Skiing
- ☐ Working on cars
- ☐ Writing
- ☐ Boating
- ☐ Motorcycling
- ☐ Horseback riding
- ☐ Tennis
- ☐ Theater
- ☐ Beach
- ☐ Volunteer work
- ☐ Singing
- ☐ Researching
- ☐ Communicating
- ☐ Treating/Caring for
- ☐ Documenting
- ☐ Maintaining
- ☐ Editing
- ☐ Reviewing
- ☐ Presenting
- ☐ Operating
- ☐ Organizing/Planning
- ☐ Resolving conflict

If there are other interests that excite you, which are not on the list above, you may add them below.

☐   ☐

☐   ☐

Choose eight key interests that excite you and write them in order.

Interest:	How it makes me feel:
1._____	_____
2._____	_____
3._____	_____
4._____	_____
5._____	_____
6._____	_____
7._____	_____
8._____	_____

Go back to the list of interests and select two new interests that you would like to explore and learn more about. Write them here.

1.   _____

2.   _____

Which of your interests are aligned with your talent?

• _____

• _____

• _____

• _____

How are those interests aligned with your talent?

1. _____
2. _____
3. _____
4. _____

Describe how you can incorporate each of your key interests in your daily life and career.

1. _____
   _____
   _____

2. _____
   _____
   _____

3. _____
   _____
   _____

4. _____
   _____
   _____

5. _____
   _____
   _____

6. _____
   _____
   _____

7. _____

_____

_____

8. _____

_____

_____

Notes

Skills

Finally, let's list your skills.

Using the following scale from 1 to 6, rank your present degree of expertise in each skill on the list below.

1. Never tried

2. Very limited

3. Below average

4. Average

5. Above average

6. Excellent

☐   Investigating— Exploring, research, study, question and/or probe for information

☐   Adding humor and fun—Contribute a funny or amusing element to an environment or process

☐   Mediating—Reconcile differences, resolve issues, conciliate and arbitrate

☐   Coaching/Counseling—Facilitate   insight,   empathize, counsel, empower, advise and guide

☐   Actively listening/Assessing needs—Tune in or pay attention in an effort to hear and understand

☐   Serving customers—Assess needs and provide appropriate goods and services. Client liaison, host events

☐   People skills—Make people talk, listen, understand and accept, sympathize, show feelings, channel anger and calm down

☐   Food preparing—Prepare ingredients, cook nutritious and tasty meals, serve and arrange food

- □ Information research—Read and use articles, books and other information sources to collect information

- □ Using technology—Use computers to treat people, process information, operate software or machinery

- □ Coordinating events—Plan and organize event details like times, facilities and agendas

- □ Analyzing—Compile, research, audit or evaluate data and/or systems and investigate

- □ Accountability/Responsibility—Be responsible for people, resources, finances and/or results

- □ Administrating—Work with systems, data and/or procedures, attend to detail

- □ Collaborating—Develop alliances and/or network, achieve with others and work in a team

- □ Managing people—Delegate authority and/or motivate others, supervise performance, design work and lead

- □ Improvising—Create spontaneously or make do with available resources

- □ Decision making—Make major, complex or frequent decisions and evaluate options

- □ Agility—Run, climb, hit, jump, dance, balance, aim, throw and catch

- □ Creative writing—Compose words, articles, stories and lyrics and write to inform or entertain others

- □ Intuition—Foresight, insight, visualize outcome

- □ Mentoring/Guiding—Guide, coach and give advice to coworkers, customers, patients, students, etc.

- □ Instructing/Supervising—Explain information and instruct/supervise students, coworkers, customers, etc.

- □ Negotiating—Reach agreements on proposals, bargain, use persuasive skills to come to terms

- □ Managing information—Record, collate, categorize, classify or record data

- Coordinating/Liaising—Represent, liaise between and act on behalf of people and groups/organizations

- Transporting—Drive vehicles, lift and load goods, carry freight and transport passengers

- Consulting—Assess clients' needs and give expert, professional advice

- Written expression—Create reports, letters, edit, correct and rewrite

- Problem solving—Diagnose factors or issues, use deductive reasoning and generate ideas

- Conflict management—Dispute arbitration and/or resolve grievances. Advocate on behalf of aggrieved parties.

- Nurturing—Treat or nurse patients; cure, heal and care for people

- Strategic thinking—Formulate objectives, set up and develop projects and plans

- Creating—Hand-make crafts: weave, carve, etc. Create art: sketch, draw, paint. Compose music.

- Conceptualizing—Visualize possibilities, generate ideas

- Managing projects—Oversee organizations and execution of tasks to achieve goals

- Motivating—Influence others, stimulate and inspire

- Making changes—Influence changes, indicate new directions and lead

- Planning—Predict requirements for events or projects, forecast and schedule

- Noticing/Observing—Study, investigate and monitor changes of patterns in work tasks and procedures, people or business operations

- Performing in public/Making presentations—Address groups of people in a public setting. Instruct, train or teach and perform.

☐ Improving—Speed up production and services, trouble-shoot, streamline processes, make work more effective

☐ Time management—Schedule meetings, set priorities

☐ Assessing situations or people—Size up a person or situation quickly and accurately

☐ Organizing—Arrange resources and schedules, implement programs or projects, prioritize actions

☐ Construction—Manufacture, assemble, erect, fabricate, create

☐ Editing/Proofreading—Edit and/or correct texts by improving language and readability

☐ Designing—Conceive, create, form a plan, project, program, product or artistic form

☐ Displaying manual dexterity—Skillful use of hands. Connecting items, materials or parts. Good eye/hand coordination.

☐ Implementing—Organize detailed structures. Implement plans, projects and/or leadership strategies. Turn theory into practice.

☐ Calculating/Computing—Count or figure amounts. Execute a mathematical process.

☐ Managing diversity—Assess new directions, cultural differences or changing work situations

☐ Follow instructions—Follow and perform detailed tasks

☐ Marketing products/services—Identify target consumers and develop strategies to sell products/services to them. Present information and convey messages.

☐ Illustrating—Draw or sketch

☐ Budgeting/Evaluating—Financial planning, cost savings, optimize use of financial and other resources and estimate values and/or costs

☐ Interviewing—Obtain information by asking the right questions

- ☐ Synthesizing—Reorganize information, integrate ideas

- ☐ Animal welfare—Breed, care for, train and show pets and other animals. Game preservation, veterinary care, prevention of cruelty to animals.

- ☐ Planting and growing—Grow fruit, vegetables, corn, flowers and trees. Sow, plant, weed, cut, harvest, etc.

- ☐ Mastering foreign languages—Being able to speak, read, understand, write and/or interpret one or more foreign languages

- ☐ Selling—Influence others to buy services, products or ideas

- ☐ Mechanical skills—Operate tools, machinery or technology. Assemble or repair

- ☐ Repairing/Renovating—Fix or restore to working condition after damage

- ☐ Measuring/Testing—Measure skills, validity, usability, quality, etc. Carry out and follow up test procedures.

If you possess skills that are not listed above, you may add them below.

- •
- •
- •
- •

Choose ten key skills that you possess and write them in the order in which you enjoy them the most.

1. _____

2. _____

3. _____

4. _____

5. _____

6. _____

7. _____

8. _____

9. _____

10. _____

Which ones are aligned with your talent?

- _____
- _____
- _____
- _____

How are those skills aligned with your talent?

- _____
- _____
- _____
- _____

What skills would you like to develop more in the future?

	Skill:	Why?
•	_____	_____
•	_____	_____
•	_____	_____
•	_____	_____

Combining your talent with your skills is your most powerful tool in life. You will always work on your craft and add to your skills. And, as long as you follow your bliss, you will be successful.

Talents

Write down your most motivating talents below. Draw a circle around each of them and brainstorm ways of using those talents. Let your mind run freely, identifying as many possibilities as you can without judging or evaluating these ideas.

For example, "Compassion" can be used in any of the following roles or ways:

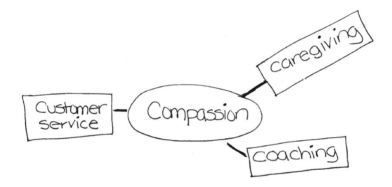

Notes

The *I*

It is time to center your awareness of "self" by writing down the founding core of who you are today. These are not merely words but are a fundamental portrayal of you. Use them as your backbone to stand up straight and face the world with clarity and purpose, because when you know who you are and what you possess, the path of your journey will be bright like the morning.

Write down your eight key values:

-
-
-
-
-
-
-
-

Write down your eight key interests:

-
-
-
-
-
-
-
-

Write down your ten key skills:

-
-
-
-
-
-
-
-
-
-

Write down your four key talents:

-
-
-
-

In all of your endeavors and adventures, always ensure that the decisions you make are aligned with who you are—that is, your values, interests, skills, and talents.

Chapter 3

Where am I going?

Create your college list

Get to know your options by visiting a college search online site where you can learn about basic collage categories and answer questions about your preferences. Write down your notes here:

Education

If achieving your goal requires education that you are lacking, applying for college might be a good path to take. It is important to be clear about what it is exactly that you would like to get out of your education before you apply to a college or university. By now, you may have a particular job in mind. It is wise to have clarity on your goal before you invest time and money in studies and to make sure that the degree will have a measurable benefit to you in pursuing your goal.

As a student, you will have opportunities to read books and attend lectures given by professors in your field of interest. This stimulation will encourage you to think, analyze, ask questions, and explore new ideas that will expand your knowledge and enhance your personal growth and development.

Remember, knowledge is the key to success. You will always need to educate yourself and acquire knowledge in order to evolve, but that doesn't mean you have to attend a college and earn a degree. You can acquire knowledge by traveling the world, reading books, and meeting people. Whatever path you choose, make sure you are clear about your intention and goal.

Let's Get Down to Business

The journey may not be easy or go exactly the way you planned, but as long as you are clear about your intentions and goals, you will travel with purpose. Keep the following advice in mind:

- Work smart and continue to hone your craft; it will pay off.
- Don't expect an outcome without putting in the work. Act on your passion!
- Always remember that the journey is your reward; success is not a destination.
- Find people who believe in you and build a good support system. You will need it!
- Find a mentor—someone who will coach you along the way.
- Don't let money distract you from your purpose.
- Don't envy others' growth; allow their success to inspire you.
- Start and end the day by taking care of yourself. Meditate and stay connected.
- Believe that you will get opportunities only when you are prepared to receive them. Keep working on your craft until you become who you need to be.
- Don't take things personally; there is a reason for everything, and it's not always about you.
- Remember that you create as you think, so focus on what will add to your growth and what you want.
- Confidence builds with practice. Take action, stand up, and show up. Dare to be confident. Dare to be you!

Professions

When you are planning your future, it is important to gather all the necessary information during the early stages of your quest to start your dream career.

Based on your talents, values, interests, and skills, circle a field or profession from the list below that you would like to learn more about to see if it might be a desirable career path for you.

List of Careers

Agriculture, Food and Natural Resources

- Agricultural Food Science Technician
- Conservation Scientist
- Environmental Engineer of Technician
- Farmer or Rancher
- Fish Hatchery Manager
- Fisher
- Food Scientist or Technologist
- Forester
- Landscaper or Groundskeeper
- Nursery of Greenhouse Manager
- Pest Control Worker
- Zoologist

Architecture and Construction

- Architect
- Carpenter
- Drafter
- Electrician
- and Air Conditioning Mechanic
- Highway Maintenance Worker
- Painter
- Plumber
- Rigger
- Roofer
- Security System Installer
- Surveyor

Arts, Audio-Video Technology and Communication

- Actor

- Art Director
- Audio or Video Equipment Technician
- Broadcast News Anchor
- Camera Operator
- Copy Writer
- Curator
- Dancer
- Desktop Publisher
- Director of Stage, Motion Pictures, Television or Radio
- Editor
- Film and Video Editor
- Graphic Designer
- Journalist
- Librarian
- Library Technician
- Multimedia Artist
- Music Director
- Musician or Singer
- Photographer
- Producer of Motion Pictures, Television or Radio
- Public Relations Specialist
- Radio or Television Announcer
- Technical Writer
- Telecommunications Line Installer and Repairer
- Usher

- Writer

Business Management and Administration

- Accountant or Auditor
- Administrative Assistant
- Budget Analyst
- Customer Service Representative
- Employment and Placement Specialist
- File Clerk
- Human Resources Assistant or Manager
- Legal Secretary
- Management Analyst
- Manager
- Medical Secretary
- Operations Research Analyst
- Proofreader
- Receptionist
- Secretary
- Statistician
- Title Examiner

Education and Training

- Education Administrator
- Elementary School Teacher
- Fitness Trainer

- Postsecondary Teacher
- School Counselor
- Secondary School Teacher
- Teacher Assistant
- Training Specialist or Manager

Finance

- Actuary
- Bill or Account Collector
- Bookkeeper
- Brokerage Clerk
- Claims Adjuster or Examiner
- Chief Financial Officer
- Credit Analyst
- Economist
- Financial Advisor
- Financial Analyst or Examiner
- Financial Manager
- Financial Services Sales Agent
- Financial Specialist
- Insurance Appraiser
- Insurance Claims Clerk
- Insurance Underwriter
- Loan Officer
- Market Research Analyst
- Payroll Clerk
- Procurement Clerk
- Tax Examiner or Collector

- Teller

Government and Public Administration

- Chief Executive
- Emergency Management Specialist
- Environmental Inspector
- Equal Opportunity Officer
- Legislator
- License Clerk
- Municipal Clerk
- Social or Community Service Manager
- Urban Planner

Health Science

- Anesthesiologist
- Athletic Trainer
- Chiropractor
- Dental Assistant or Hygienist
- Dentist
- Dietitian or Nutritionist
- Doctor
- Emergency Medical Technician
- Licensed Practical Nurse
- Massage Therapist
- Medical or Health Services Manager

- Medical Assistant
- Medical Records Technician
- Occupational Therapist
- Optometrist
- Orthodontist
- Pharmacist
- Pharmacy Technician
- Physical Therapist
- Physician's Assistant
- Podiatrist
- Psychiatrist
- Radiologic Technician
- Recreational Therapist
- Registered Nurse
- Respiratory Therapist
- Surgeon
- Speech-Language Pathologist
- Veterinarian
- Veterinarian Assistant

Hospitality and Tourism

- Amusement and Recreation Attendant
- Bellhop
- Bartender
- Chef
- Coach or Scout
- Cook

- Dishwasher
- Food Preparation Worker
- Food Service Manager
- Gaming or Sports Book Writer
- Gaming Cage Worker
- Gaming Dealer
- Gaming Manager
- Hotel Desk Clerk
- Maid or Housekeeper
- Recreation Worker
- Tour Guide
- Travel Agent
- Umpire or Referee
- Waiter or Waitress

Human Services

- Child Care Worker
- Clergy
- Clinical Psychologist
- Counselor
- Educational Psychologist
- Marriage and Family Therapist
- Probation Officer
- Social Worker
- Sociologist
- Substance Abuse Counselor

Information Technology

- Computer and Information Science Manager
- Computer Programmer
- Computer Security Specialist
- Computer Software Engineer
- Computer Support Specialist
- Computer Systems Analyst
- Database Administrator
- Network Administrator
- Website Developer

Law, Public Safety and Security

- Aircrew Officer
- Animal Control Worker
- Court Clerk
- Court Reporter
- Detective
- Fire Inspector
- Firefighter
- Immigration or Customs Inspector
- Judge
- Lawyer
- Paralegal
- Police Officer
- Private Detective
- Security Guard

Manufacturing

- Avionics Technician
- Baker
- Boilermaker
- Carpenter
- Civil Engineering Technician
- Commercial Driver
- Electrical Engineer or Technician
- Gem or Diamond Worker
- Glass Blower
- Home Appliance Repairer
- Locksmith
- Machinist
- Medical Equipment Repairer
- Model Maker
- Molding or Casting Worker
- Purchasing Agent
- Sewing Machine Operator
- Tool or Die Maker
- Upholsterer
- Welder

Marketing, Sales and Service

- Advertising Manager
- Appraiser
- Barber
- Butcher

- Cashier
- Fashion Designer
- Funeral Director
- Hairdresser
- Interior Designer
- Jeweler
- Makeup Artist
- Marketing Manager
- Model
- Real Estate Agent or Broker
- Retail Salesperson
- Sales Manager
- Sales Representative
- Telemarketer

Science, Technology and Engineering

- Aerospace Engineer
- Archeologist
- Astronomer
- Atmospheric Scientist
- Biologist
- Cartographer
- Chemical Engineer
- Chemist
- Civil Engineer
- Engineering Manager
- Environmental Scientist

- Forensic Technician
- Geographer
- Industrial Engineer
- Marine Engineer
- Materials Engineer
- Mechanical Engineer
- Nuclear Engineer
- Oceanographer
- Physicist

Transportation and Distribution

- Air Traffic Controller
- Aircraft Mechanic
- Airline Pilot
- Automotive Body Repairer
- Automotive Mechanic
- Bus Driver
- Captain or Pilot of Water Vessels
- Dispatcher
- Flight Attendant
- Locomotive Engineer
- Motorboat Mechanic
- Motorcycle Mechanic
- Postal Service Mail Carrier
- Taxi Driver
- Transportation Manager
- Truck Driver

If you have another profession in mind that is not listed above, you may add it below.

-
-
-
-

1. What jobs interest you, and where do you think you can contribute your talent, skills, and interests the most?

- _____
- _____
- _____
- _____
- _____
- _____
- _____
- _____
- _____

2. Which professions would you like to get more information about?

- _____
- _____
- _____
- _____
- _____

Chapter 4

How do I get there?

Success Stories

Take a moment and think of all the things you have done in your life that resulted in a positive outcome. Perhaps you contributed to your community by doing volunteer work, improved your sales at work, succeeded in your studies, assisted family members, or made achievements in sports. Your stories can relate to your hobbies, work, leisure, philanthropy, school, and more.

Describe your success stories and what you have accomplished. Give short examples and focus on the results. Use the following template:

- Problem: *The boutique could not sell clothes from the sales rack.*
- Activity: *I organized the clothes by size and color.*
- Result: *Sales increased, as it became easier for the customers to see and appreciate the different styles.*

Keep it short—one sentence per line.

Your success stories can add tremendous value to your résumé and job interviews. You can use them as concrete examples of how you solve problems and help develop your work assignments. They are inspiring stories that will give a prospective employer insight into who you are.

P: _____

A: _____

R: _____

P: _____

A: _____

R: _____

P: _____

A: _____

R: _____

P: _____

A: _____

R: _____

Notes

Networking

One of the best ways to find out about careers that appeal to you, and also to build professional relationships, is through networking. It is the most powerful marketing tactic for accelerating and sustaining success—because, ultimately, it's not about who you know but who knows you.

Map out Your Network

Advantages like jobs or business opportunities can be established and seized when you network and maintain informal relationships. Simply put, networking means having a dialogue and building relationships. It is a great way to receive information about what excites and interests you and, at the same time, present yourself and your ideas and desires for your future.

Your network consists of people who, in one way or another, have come in contact with you throughout your life, such as family, friends, and teachers. These contacts can be of different ages, levels of education, and levels of responsibility, and they can live anywhere in the world. Practice the following skills to succeed in your networking:

- Smile! Enjoy the moment.
- Be a friend first. Do your best to help others when you can.
- Be real. People can feel when you aren't being yourself. Make sure that you represent your true self in all of your encounters with others.
- Believe that you are good enough! Know your worth and be proud of who you are and what you have to offer.

Why You Should Network

Network so that you can

- choose a profession or a direction in your career
- find the hidden jobs
- make new job and career opportunities
- get information about different work fields and jobs
- get help preparing your job-seeking plan and job-seeking tools
- find a job
- find people who can help you along the way
- get emotional support
- get help making decisions, if you are starting your own business
- develop your business
- succeed in your current job

What are the benefits of networking?

- You will become more skilled and confident in the course of gathering information.
- You will obtain knowledge of the job market by conversing with people in your desired field.
- You will find out which companies are hiring and where the available jobs are.

Make an inventory of your network

Where can you find your contacts? Here are a few suggestions. Place a checkmark next to each category in which you know people who have careers or connections that would be of interest to you, and add their names to the list.

Leisure

- ☐ Family _____
- ☐ Relatives _____
- ☐ Your partner _____
- ☐ Your partner's family and friends _____
- ☐ Friends, their family and colleagues _____
- ☐ Acquaintances Sports clubs _____
- ☐ Your gym _____
- ☐ Neighbors _____
- ☐ HOA or property manager _____
- ☐ Your child's friends and their families _____
- ☐ Parents and teachers at your child's school _____
- ☐ Your veterinarian _____
- ☐ Your doctor _____
- ☐ Your dentist _____
- ☐ Your banker _____
- ☐ Churches, temples, mosques or any other religious or spiritual location _____
- ☐ Golf and boat clubs _____
- ☐ Your travels _____
- ☐ Cab driver _____
- ☐ Bus driver _____
- ☐ Your favorite restaurant _____
- ☐ Housekeeper _____
- ☐ Nanny _____
- ☐ Spa/Nail salon/ Hairdresser _____
- ☐ Therapist/Coach/Psychologist _____
- ☐ Associations _____

People whom you...
- ☐ Dated _____
- ☐ Met at someone's house _____
- ☐ Say hi to on your daily travels _____
- ☐ Work out with _____
- ☐ Receive email and letters from (holiday, birthday cards, etc.) _____
- ☐ Chat with _____
- ☐ Go out to bars or clubs with _____
- ☐ Share hobbies with _____
- ☐ Share membership in a network with _____
- ☐ Are connected to on social media (Facebook, Instagram, LinkedIn, Twitter, etc.) _____

Current and previous jobs
- ☐ Current colleagues _____
- ☐ Previous coworkers _____
- ☐ Managers/Bosses _____
- ☐ Clients/Customers _____
- ☐ Suppliers _____
- ☐ Professional contacts _____
- ☐ Freelancers _____
- ☐ Contacts within the industry _____
- ☐ Retailers _____
- ☐ Contacts from previous job searches _____
- ☐ Banks, lawyers and accountants _____

Education and courses
- ☐ Classmates _____
- ☐ Night classes _____
- ☐ Teachers _____

☐ Lecturers _____

☐ Internal trainers at previous jobs _____

☐ Counselors and Career advisors/coaches _____

How many networking groups do you have? _____

Notes

The Consultation Interview

Once you have clarity on your network, it will be time for you to reach out and gather information. The most valuable approach to collecting information about a job that interests you is to talk to someone who is working in the field. Think of this as an interview that you're conducting with an employer to gain firsthand knowledge of the workplace and the job requirements, to build your professional network, and to market and present yourself.

This approach is a different but highly effective way of forging your dream career. You choose the field of work that you are curious about and reach out to employers to get the information you need before you go ahead and apply for the job. When you know what you have to offer and are confident in your intention to serve, you can approach the employer to see if the organization is a good match for you, your values, and your interests.

NOTE! The interview should not take more than 20–30 minutes!

1. Choose several jobs that interest you. I recommend at least five.

2. Do research about the company and each position that piques your interest.

3. Write down the questions you have about each job. Try to ask questions that will provide the clarity you need. Remember that the job you choose should always be aligned with your talents, values, interests, and goals.

4. Start by interviewing three people you know. That will allow you to practice before you meet with people you don't know.

5. Decide whom you would like to interview. Contact that person via e-mail or phone to schedule an appointment.

Whom to interview?

To obtain the correct information about your career goals and paths, you must choose the right person to contact. Make a list of individuals here. Remember that you may have to contact one person in order to get referred to another person who can give you the information you need.

Interesting jobs	Contacts	Time of info-interview	Done
1.	1. 2. 3. 4. 5.		
2.	1. 2. 3. 4. 5.		
3.	1. 2. 3. 4. 5.		
4.	1. 2. 3. 4. 5.		

5.	1. 2. 3. 4. 5.		

Notes

Prepare Your Approach

When the time comes to make the phone calls and send out e-mails to book the interviews, you will benefit from having a script ready. Make sure that your script adheres to the following formula:

- Ask for help! People love to feel like they are helping others.
    - o *I'd appreciate your help…*
    - o *I hope you will be able to guide me…*
- Offer clarity! Be specific about what you are asking for.
    - o *I would like to know about how you got started and what it is like to work at your company.*
    - o *I am interested in hearing your perspective on this industry.*
- Share your inspiration! Share your passion for the career path or the company.
    - o *I am reaching out to you specifically because…*
- Be considerate! Honor their time and make sure they feel appreciated.
    - o *Twenty minutes of your time would be very valuable to me.*

Write your script

Dear Mrs./Mr.…
My name is… _____

_____

_____

_____

_____

_____

_____

_____

The Approach (Scheduled Meeting)

1. First, briefly share your purpose and what you hope to get out of the meeting—namely, information about what it is like to work for that company. You want to know what it would be like to "walk in their shoes" for a day, to see if the company or the particular role of the person you are interviewing aligns with your professional interest. Be nice, respectful, and purposeful.

2. Ask questions that you have prepared specifically for the person you are interviewing.

3. Remember that the intention is not to apply for these jobs but to gather enough information to help in making a career-related decision.

4. At the end of each consultation, ask if the contact can refer you to someone from their network, whom you could speak with next.

5. Right after each consultation, write a summary of the information given to you. That way, you will not forget what was said.

6. Always send an e-mail within 24 hours to follow up with each individual whom you have interviewed. That will show your appreciation; everyone likes to be acknowledged. The intention is to leave a good impression of yourself and to make it easier for you to reach out to them for guidance in the future.

7. After you have done a couple of interviews, it will be time to do a breakdown of the information that you have gathered. This will allow you to remove from the list the jobs that do not align with your professional interests.

8. Choose the jobs that excite you and your soul and that are aligned with your talent and purpose.

9. Follow up with all of the contacts that you have made and share your progress with them; this is a great way to complete the circle of acquaintance with each of them.

10. When you have gathered all of the important information about what it takes to secure the job you desire, then you can start sketching out the foundation of your future resume and cover letter.

Job Search

Self-Marketing

Marketing yourself will help you build the career you desire. Writing a résumé and cover letter enables you to present an image of yourself as an employee. It gives you an opportunity to effectively communicate your values, skills, experiences, and vision to potential employers. Successful self-marketing helps you separate yourself from the hundreds of other applicants who may be competing for the same job.

The Cover Letter

A cover letter is written to highlight your qualifications for the job for which you are applying. It provides the employer with a synopsis of the reasons why you are a good candidate. The goal of the cover letter is very simple: to make a positive first impression, so that you are granted the opportunity of attending a job interview.

Before you start your cover letter, prepare answers to the following questions:

- What excites me about this job?
- What is my interest in this specific company?

- What can I contribute to this job and the company?
- What have I learned from my previous work experience (including school/internships) that the employer may find interesting?

Draw from those answers as you follow these steps to write your cover letter:

1. Introduce yourself.

2. Make a positive first impression.

   a. Generate interest in reading your résumé with a powerful opening, such as the following: *It excites me to find an opening for [the position you are applying for] with [company name] because your work with [describe the company's mission] has been important to me for a long time. I am the perfect candidate for this position because it combines my talents, values, skills, and goals with [title of position or task].*

   b. Present yourself as a suitable candidate for the job. Sell yourself! Share your talents, values, and skills, and describe how they are aligned with the position.

3. Show your professionalism.

   a. Demonstrate professional writing skills by writing an excellent cover letter. Don't be afraid to ask for help. Look through your network and see if you know someone with writing skills and experience.

   b. Emphasize your qualifications and experience by sharing how you can help the company grow and achieve its goals.

   c. Share your excitement about, and interest in, an opportunity to meet and discuss the position.

The Résumé

A résumé is a brief account of a person's education, qualifications, and previous experience. This document lists your employment history. It summarizes the jobs you have had; your education, certifications, and skills; and other applicable information about your background. Follow these ten steps when writing your résumé:

1. Find a job first and then write a new résumé for that specific job. Don't make the mistake of looking for the job *after* writing your résumé.

2. List keywords for your résumé. Recruiters and employers search for keywords that are relevant to the particular job requirements, so you need to put them in your résumé if you want to be noticed. For an administrative assistant, for example, keywords include *attention to detail, customer service, organized, managing databases,* and *juggling competing priorities.*

3. Choose a résumé format. Keep it professional.

4. Your résumé heading is just an inch of text, but it says a lot about you, so make sure you do it the right way: name, address, e-mail, phone number, and website (if applicable).

5. Your résumé objective is a short target statement that outlines the direction of your career. This will provide clarity to the employer and position you as a perfect match for the job requirements.

6. In the summary of your qualifications, make sure to provide the employer with the very best of what you have to offer.

7. Make the best of your work history; make it relevant to the job for which you are applying.

8. Outline your success stories in your résumé as achievement statements. Write three sentences describing what the

problem was, what you did to solve it, and the positive results of your initiative. Success stories tell the employer you're worth hiring—or at least worth interviewing.

9. Highlight your education on the résumé. If you are a recent graduate or have fewer than five years of work experience, place education before experience. Education should also come first if you are changing careers and have continued your education to support your new goal or if you have five or more years of experience related to your goal.

10. List community service and other volunteer work on your résumé, if you believe that it makes a statement about your dedication, character, or social awareness—or if it in any way enhances your qualifications for the job.

Before submitting your résumé, go over the following checklist to make it perfect:

Layout

- Is my name at the top of the page and in bold?
- Are my address, phone number, and e-mail accurate?
- Is my résumé an appropriate length? (One page is preferred.)
- Is the formatting (e.g., bold, font, bullet, and heading styles) consistent throughout the résumé? Are the headings and statements evenly spaced?

Content

- Does my objective statement clearly state what I am seeking and what I will offer to the position?
- Have I included the following headings: Education, Experience, and Skills?

- Does my education section state my official degree and expected graduation date? Have I included my cumulative GPA?
- Do my statements demonstrate accomplishments, rather than routine tasks and duties?
- Do my accomplishment statements demonstrate the use of my key skills?
- Do my statements demonstrate the results of my accomplishments? Have I quantified my results? (e.g., using numbers when possible)
- Is my résumé completely free from spelling, punctuation, and grammatical errors?

Fine-Tuning

- Sleep on it.
- Read through and make changes.
- Let at least three other people read your résumé and give you feedback.

Link Up through LinkedIn

LinkedIn is a networking website designed specifically for the business community. The goal of the site is to allow you to establish fruitful relationships and develop your professional network.

LinkedIn is a great resource to take advantage of when you are seeking to advance your career. The first step is to create an attractive and interesting profile, where you convey your current and former professional roles. Your profile page should emphasize your talents, skills, employment history, and education. But do not confuse your LinkedIn profile with a formal résumé that is designed to attract the attention of an employer and initiate an interview.

Your LinkedIn profile is social, and the website should be used as a platform for networking and interacting with a wide variety of people. Use the website to share what you care about as a professional and build relationships with people who are in a position to have a great impact on your job hunt and career growth. While you can use LinkedIn to apply for specific jobs, I encourage you to appreciate the website's networking opportunity, as it will assist you in your professional growth. The larger your network becomes, the greater the chances will be for you to come in contact with someone relevant to your dream career.

A great way to break the ice while you are networking on LinkedIn is to incorporate a reference to something you've learned about the person or the company by reading their profile page. There are many advantages to using LinkedIn, so take some time to do research on the website. The knowledge you have gained from completing the exercises in this book has already prepared you to create your profile page.

Notes

Job Research and Analysis

Always make sure that you read a job ad in full and understand the requirements of the company and the position. Highlight the necessary qualifications and write them down. In addition, write down the ways in which you are suitable for the job. Before you apply, you must analyze how well you fit with what it takes to get the job and how you can contribute with your skills and talents.

Job qualifications	How to match them
1.	
2.	

Job Interview

A job interview has two purposes: It offers the employer valuable insight into your personality and abilities, and it allows you to recognize whether your talents, values, and career goals match up with what the company is seeking. The job interview is the perfect occasion to demonstrate good manners and your ability to articulate thoughts and ideas. Interviewers want to know why hiring you will benefit the company, so hype your achievements by sharing your success stories.

Talk about your career goals. Share your vision, describe where you are headed, and find out if the company's goals align with yours. This will show the interviewer that you are motivated by a purpose and are career-driven—two traits that are attractive to any company.

Get as much information as possible from the person interviewing you. Let him or her inform you about the job duties and what is expected of the company and its culture. Listen to understand what the company really values and expects from its employees. Based on what you are seeing and hearing, is this a place where you could thrive and be engaged and at ease?

The following are some typical interview questions:

- **Can you tell me a little about yourself?** This question seems simple, but it's crucial. Your response to this request will set the tone of the rest of the interview. Share the qualities that are beneficial and relevant to the position you are seeking. Make sure that you have done your research into the qualities the company is looking for.
- **How did you hear about the position?** If you were referred to apply for this position by doing a consultation interview or if you know someone relevant to the company, you should share the contact's name. If you applied via a website or an ad, specify why the role or job caught your attention.

- **What do you know about the company?** In asking this question, the employer is not hoping for you to quote the company's "About" page but, instead, to share whether you understand and care about the intention behind the company's goals and mission.
- **Why do you want this job?** Explain how your values and interests align with the employer's. Share what excites you about the job and how you can serve through your talents.
- **Why should we hire you?** You have shared your values and interests. Now it is time to share your skills and how they match the company's requirements. Make sure you are clear about how each of your skills can contribute and yield great results for the job, the team, and the company's culture.
- **What are your greatest professional strengths?** Share your talents and skills, combined with your ability to learn and grow. Do not say what you think the employer wants to hear. Dare to be *you*.
- **What do you consider to be your weaknesses?** It is important to stay professional and not take this question personally. Strike a balance by sharing something that you struggle with, but are working to improve. You can take examples from the skills exercise and share those that you want to improve.
- **What is your greatest professional achievement?** Don't be shy when answering this question. Share your success story, no matter how big or small it is. Share it with a smile and be proud.
- **Tell me about a challenge or conflict you've faced at work and how you dealt with it.** In asking this question, your interviewer wants to get a sense of how you will respond to conflict. You can use a success story, focusing on how you handled the situation professionally, ideally closing with a happy ending (e.g., how you brought about a resolution to a conflict at work or compromise).

- **Where do you see yourself in five years?** Share your ambitions for the future and align the position you are applying for with your goals and aspirations. If the position is a quick stepping stone to your goals, explain that you are not quite sure what the future holds, but that you see this experience playing a valuable role in helping you make that decision.

- **What is your dream job?** Again, talk about your goals and ambitions—and how this job will get you closer to them.

- **What are you looking for in a new position?** Hint: Ideally, what you are looking for should be the same things that this position has to offer. Be specific.

- **How do you deal with pressure or stressful situations?** This is a great way to share your understanding that when life happens, it is your reaction to the situation that ultimately brings about the outcome, whether positive or negative. Share that you react to pressure not with stress but by focusing on the task at hand, using your energy to create a positive outcome, confident that you are doing your best—which is all that matters in the end.

- **What are your salary requirements?** It is important that you know your own worth and the value of your time. But you have to be reasonable and know the market, so do some research by visiting websites that can give you relevant figures. In this way, you will likely come up with a range. Base that range on what you are now clear about: your values, skills, and experience. Make sure the hiring manager knows that you are willing to negotiate.

- **What do you like to do outside of work?** This is a great way to share your interests. Your interviewer will see a part of your personality and recognize that you are a great candidate, who will fit into the company's culture.

- **Do you have any questions for us?** This is your opportunity to get some insight into the position, the company, the department, and the team. Use some of the questions from the consultation interviews, such as "What's your favorite part about working here?" or "What can you tell me about your new products or plans for growth?" This is another way for you to show your interest in the company.

Final Thoughts

I hope that by reading this book and completing the exercises, you have gained more clarity on your *I* in life.

We all want to be happy and successful, but it is up to us to take charge of our lives. I believe that we are obligated to live life while serving to the fullest of our potential—obligated to ourselves as individuals and as human beings who are part of a divine evolution.

I will end this book by sharing something that is sacred to me and close to my heart. I have been honored and blessed to have a strong, loving, and caring family and friends, who have shared not only their love and support but also their divine wisdom with me throughout my life. This wisdom has helped shed light on my journey in life, and I hope that it does the same for you.

I asked my family and friends to go back to their younger selves and give one piece of advice that they believe would have created clarity on their *I* in life—if they had known then what they know now. The following is what they had to share.

Ryan, 36: *"Be aware of other people's intentions,
let them be aligned with yours."*

Marjan, 33: *"Dare to be different."*

Sosso, 32: *"Choose your friends wisely."*

Freddi, 39: *"Laugh and have fun."*

Donya, 32: *"Listen to the advice you get from loved ones."*

Crystal, 31: "*Believe in yourself and know that you are a beautiful work of art handcrafted by God.*"

Reza, 66: "*Follow your talent and passion for music. SING your heart out!*"

Sholeh 54: "*Be honest with yourself; always face the truth, no matter how hard it is.*"

Azar, 55: "*If life doesn't go your way, know that you have the power to turn it around. Face your life with bravery.*"

Ilnaz, 31: "*Don't grow up too fast; everything has its own time. Enjoy being a teenager.*"

Amin, 31: "*Be brave. Life is a beautiful ride, and on that ride, always put your family first.*"

Lucie, 25: "*You will get over him, girl; trust me.*"

Farzan, 29: "*Don't quit pursuing your talent; keep on doing it until you overcome the roadblocks and succeed with your passion.*"

Mojdeh, 49: "*Don't be so sensitive and fragile; build on your character so that you won't be affected easily by negative words and actions.*"

Negin, 26: "*Have fun, because every moment you waste on worrying and being afraid is a wasted moment that could have been a precious memory.*"

Liah, 31: "*Don't fear the big world, for it gets smaller as you build your confidence and pursue your dreams.*"

Nina, 31: *"You can be anything you want to be or have anything you want to have in life, as long as you believe in yourself. If you don't believe in yourself, no one else will either."*

Mojgan, 53: *"Happiness comes from within you and should not be affected by situations, material things, and other people."*

Sally, 29: *"Trust and have faith in yourself."*

Rana, 35: *"Don't worry; it will all be okay! I promise."*

Paulina, 31: *"Don't regret your past. Embrace and be proud of the shadow that follows you throughout your life."*

Rally, 30: *"Surround yourself with friends that will help uplift your spirit."*

Rody, 48: *"Stop to enjoy each and every moment in your life."*

Shapour, 50: *"Spend your days doing what makes you happy, so that you can live life with meaning and purpose."*

Maja, 35: *"Inside of you, there is a primal force, and you should treat it as your best friend. Do not choke; nourish and listen to it, and it will help you take on life with greatness."*

Mehran, 48: *"Continue your education; work and stand on your own feet. Invest your time in building yourself."*

Alaleh, 34: *"Set high goals and be the best you can be."*

Behnam, 58: *"Invest your time in doing what you are passionate about."*

Mona, 35: *"Don't turn your back on subjects that do not pique your interest in school; challenge yourself by expanding your knowledge."*

Bozana, 40: *"Be in touch with your passion and true calling, as it will keep you alive."*

Merran, 28: *"There are no unreachable goals; you are the only one limiting yourself. Aim high and believe that you can do it."*

Nahid, 56: *"Continue your education based on your passion and talent."*

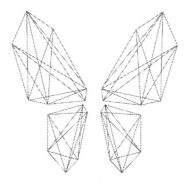